THE HEALING HEART

The Healing Heart

a collection on canvas

ALEIYA HUNTER

Dendera Publishing

CONTENTS

Aleiya Hunter spent her childhood in the United States in the New England countryside, where she enjoyed a deep connection with nature and animals...bunnies, horses, chasing butterflies, climbing trees, picking wild-flowers and blackberries, spending fascinated hours playing with fireflies and star-gazing.

There was nothing easy or simple for a "sensitive" child living with parents that lacked the understanding and capacity to nurture beyond fear and anger. The elemental kingdom (and a pair of Pisces grandmothers), offered her friendships, magic, and sanctuary to keep the child in human form alive. As her life progressed, she would walk distinctly in two separate worlds. A university educated and national award-winning communications specialist, photographer and consultant on a corporate-business path paralleled a steady progression in learning who and what she was. An intuitive capable of integrating energy work and communication thru multiple dimensions.

With more than 30-years' experience and a foundation in the primary areas of metaphysics including astrology, energy work, universal law, meditation, kinesiology, mediumship, numerology, divination systems, crystals and more; Aleiya now works at the planetary level with a diverse team of non-physical guides from the galactic, angelic and elemental realms. Whether as a classroom instructor, artist, or in providing individual guidance, their goal is to demonstrate the successful integration and positive outcomes that can happen by understanding the application in daily life of how energy, intuition, manifestation, and universal law can work hand-in-hand in practical decision-making to bring peace, solutions and graceful transformation.

Aleiya provides expanded discussions thru *the Dendera Gateway* on the latest energy shifts and world events, in addition to specific tips and tools to assist in balancing as well as navigating both personal and global changes. Her energy artwork can be viewed though *Dendera Impressions* gallery.

www.DenderaPublishing.com

www.DenderaImpressions.com

INTRODUCTION

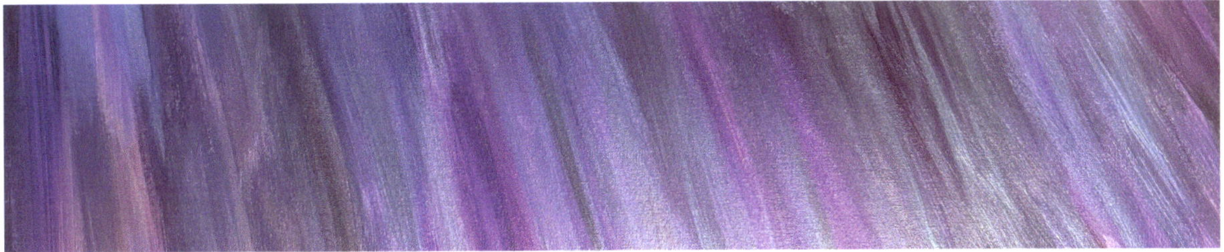

"Standing at a turning point for an age of humanity, an invitation is presented, and an inevitable change is upon the world. A heart opening that includes the opportunity to bring finality to any wounding that has been embedded in the body, mind, and spirit. The earth and all the beings who walk here will now encounter a great shift." ~ Guides to Aleiya

Original artwork by intuitive, author and teacher, Aleiya Hunter; featuring a collection of (27) acrylic on canvas paintings. Each embedded with the energetics to assist in the healing and upliftment of both the heart and life path.

BLUE FIRE

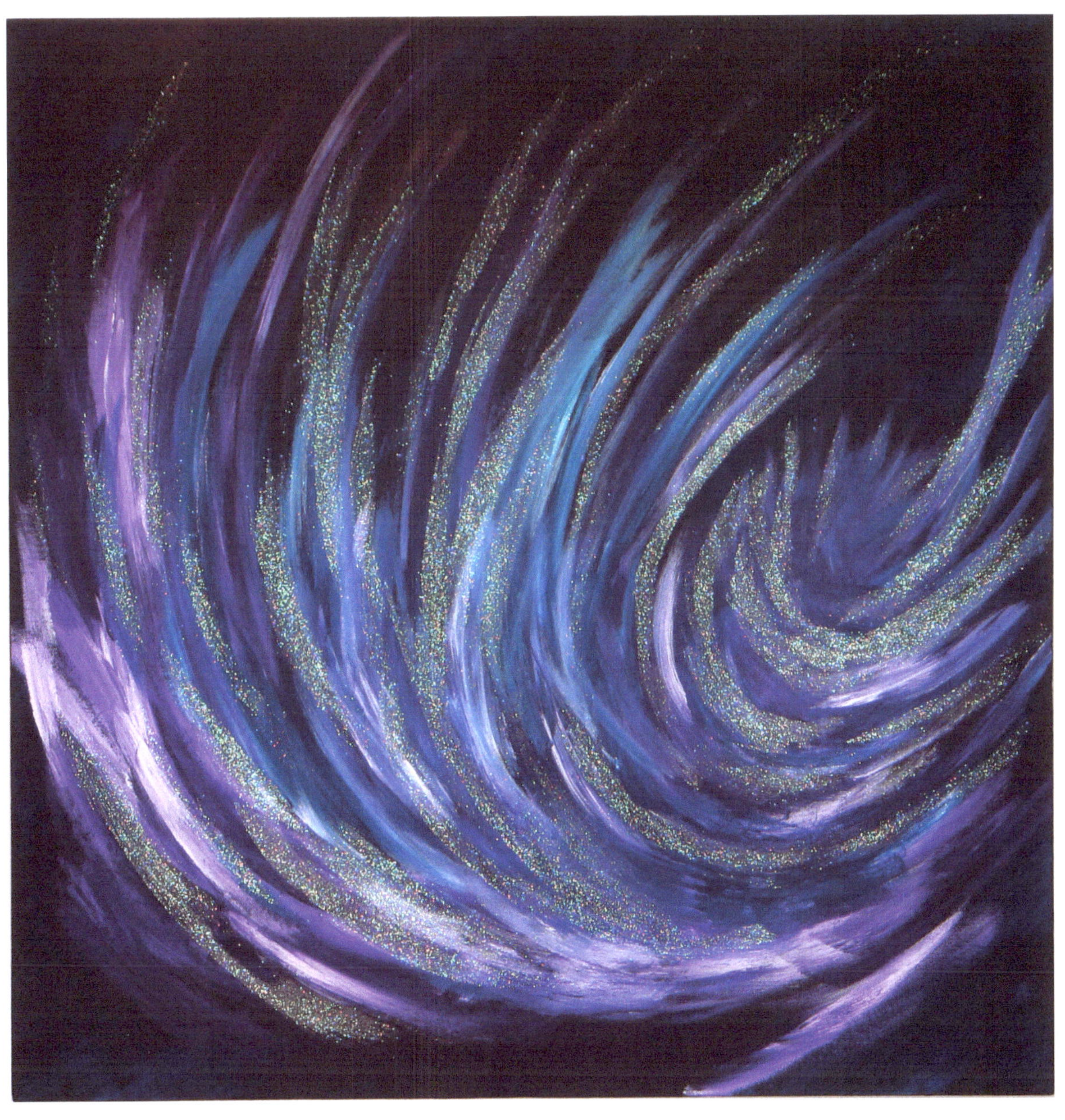

DRAGON ENERGY

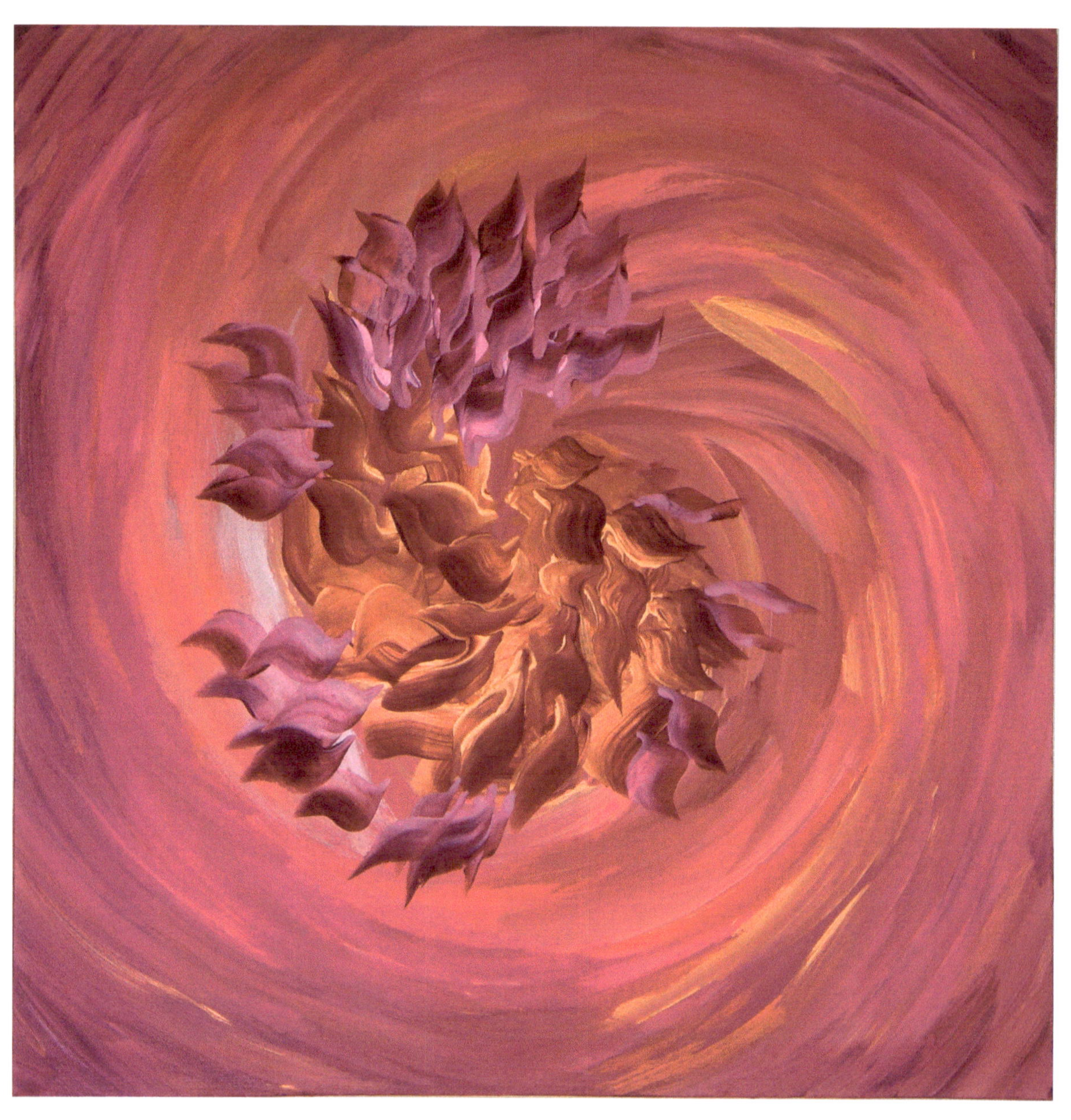

THE GATHERING

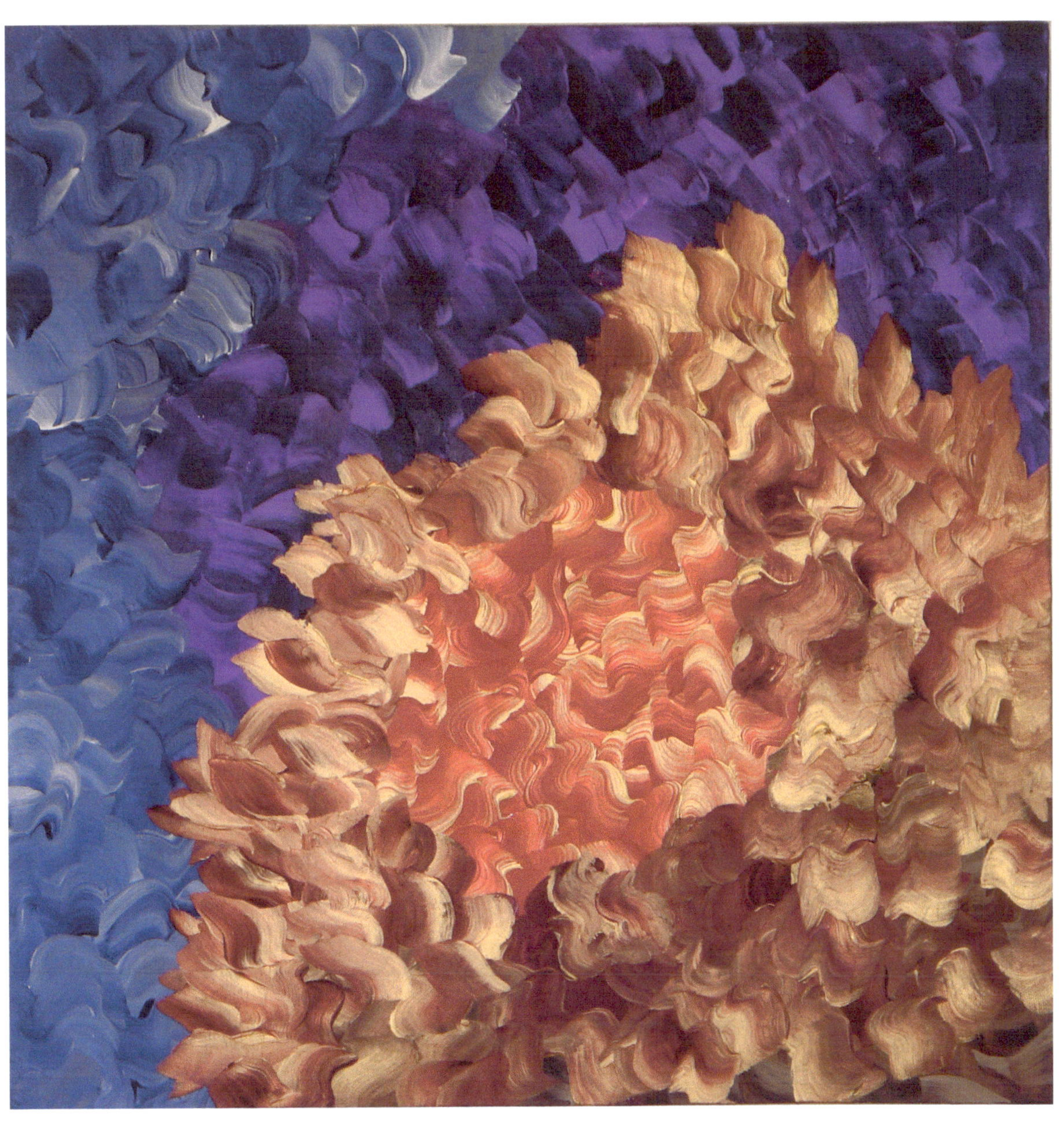

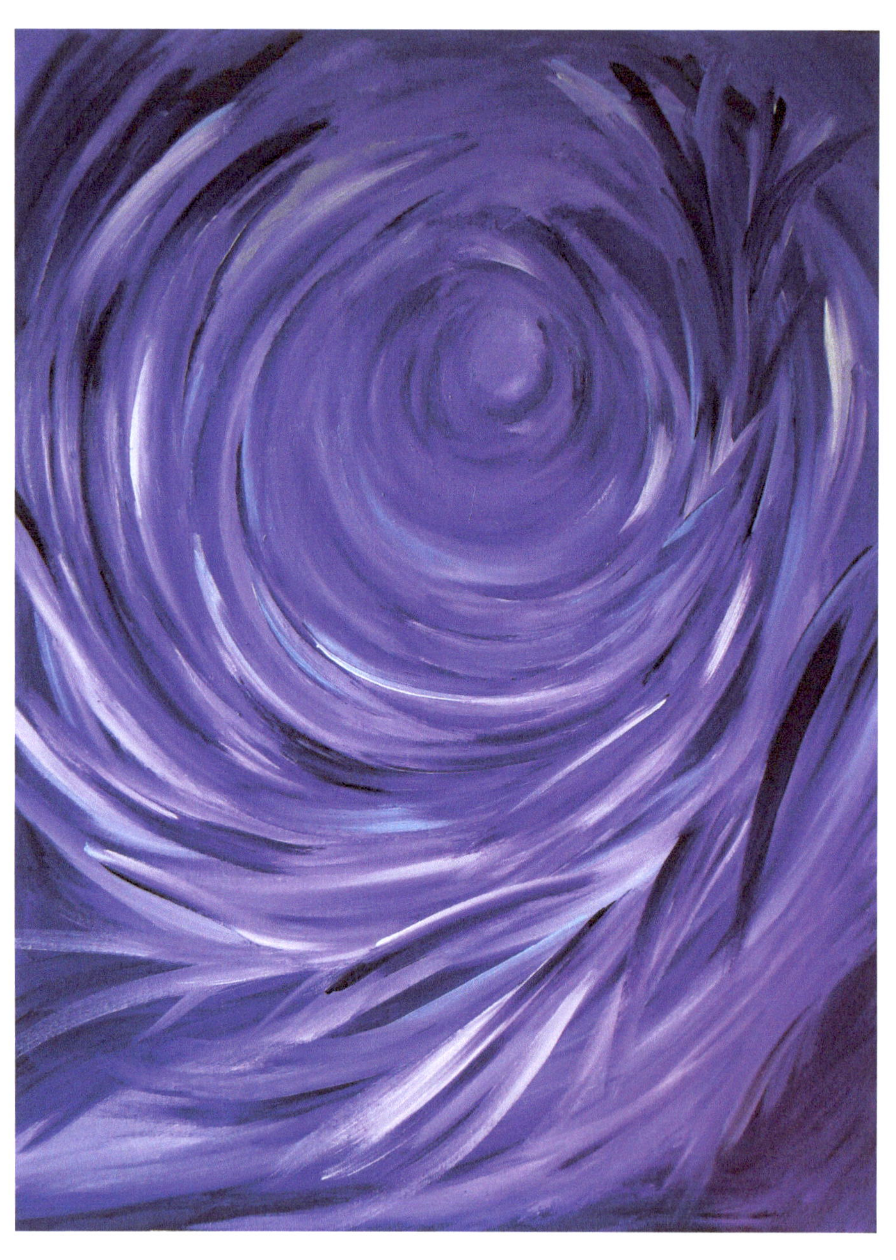

BLUE PORTAL

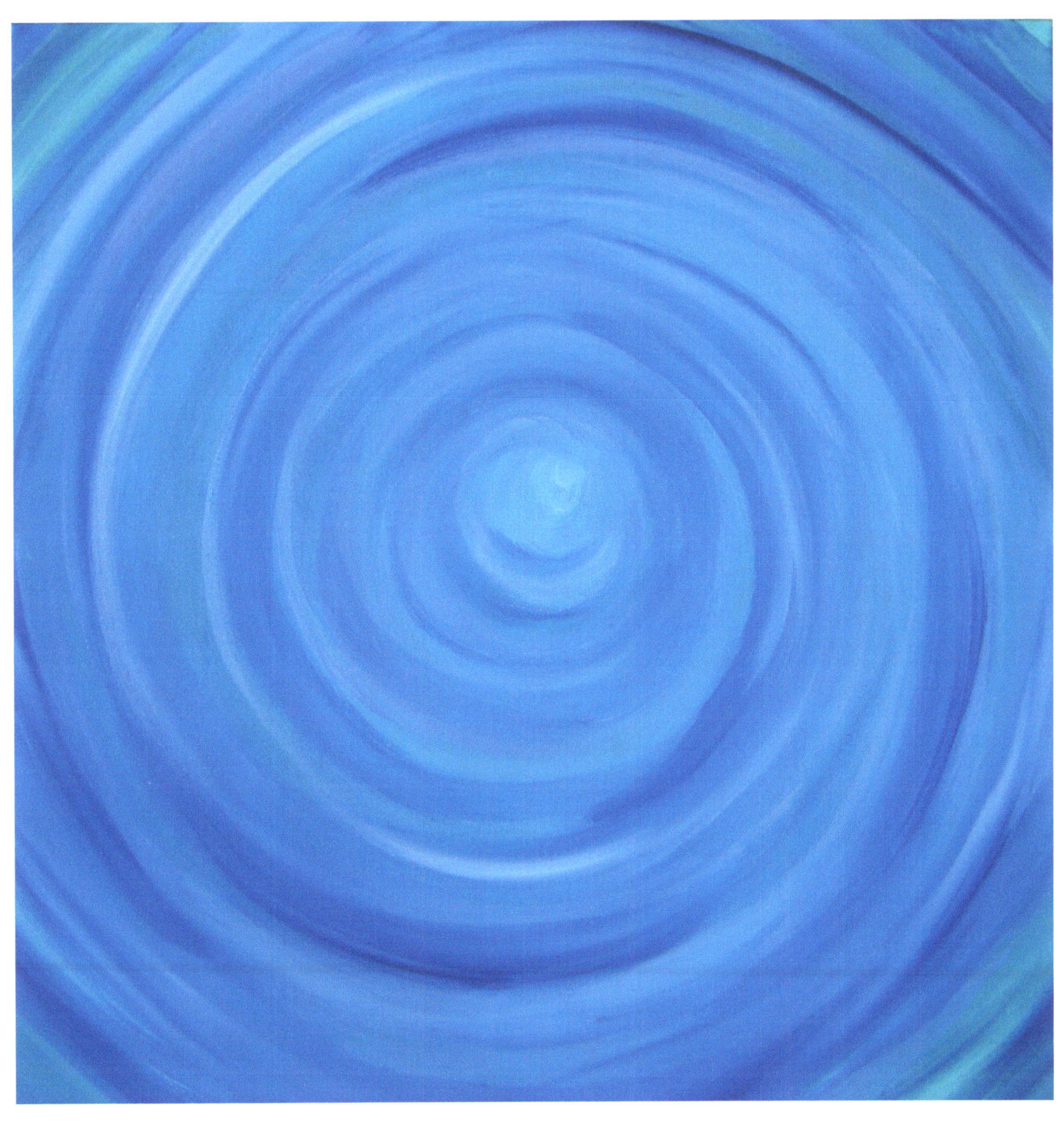

EMERGENCE

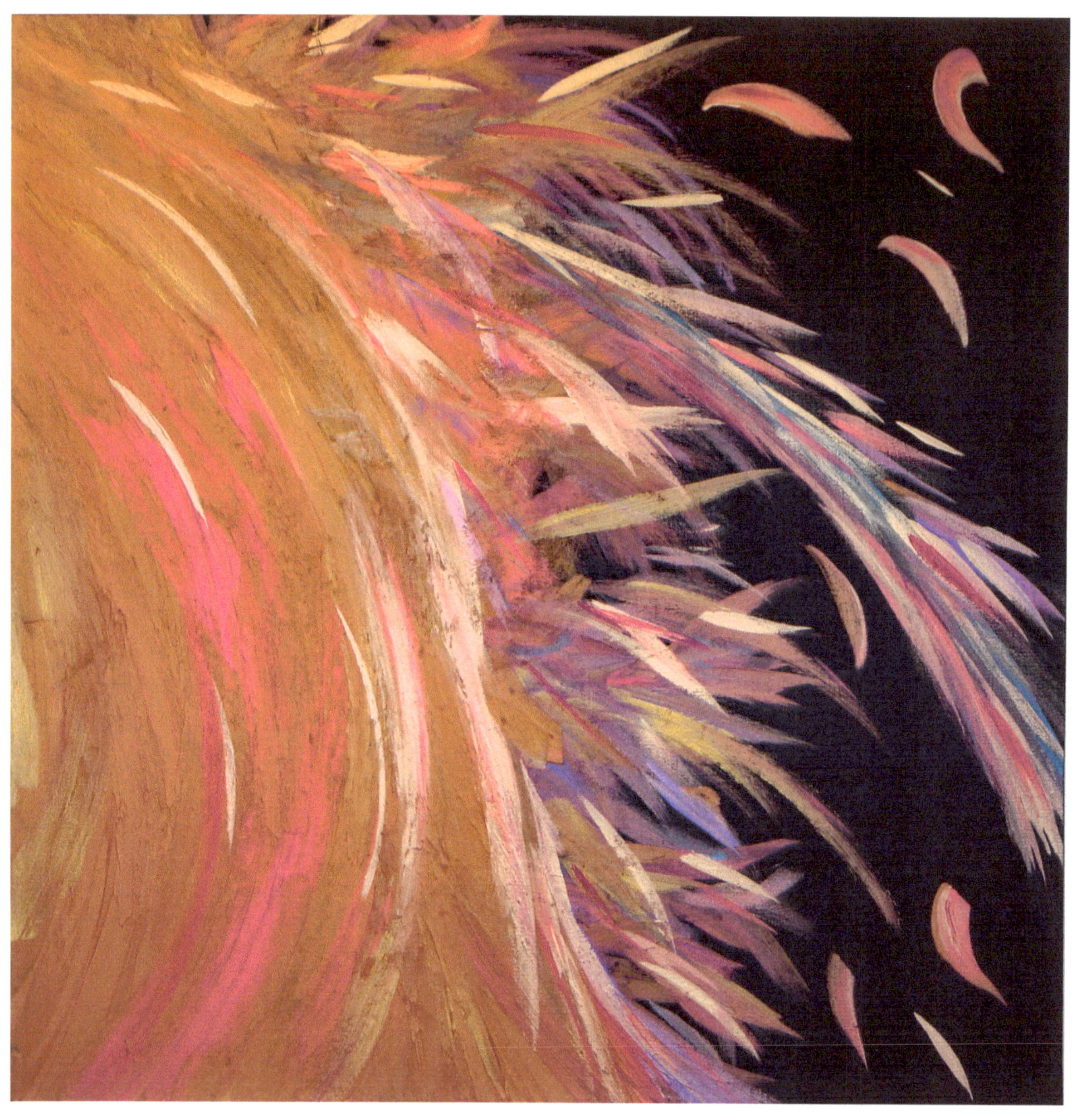

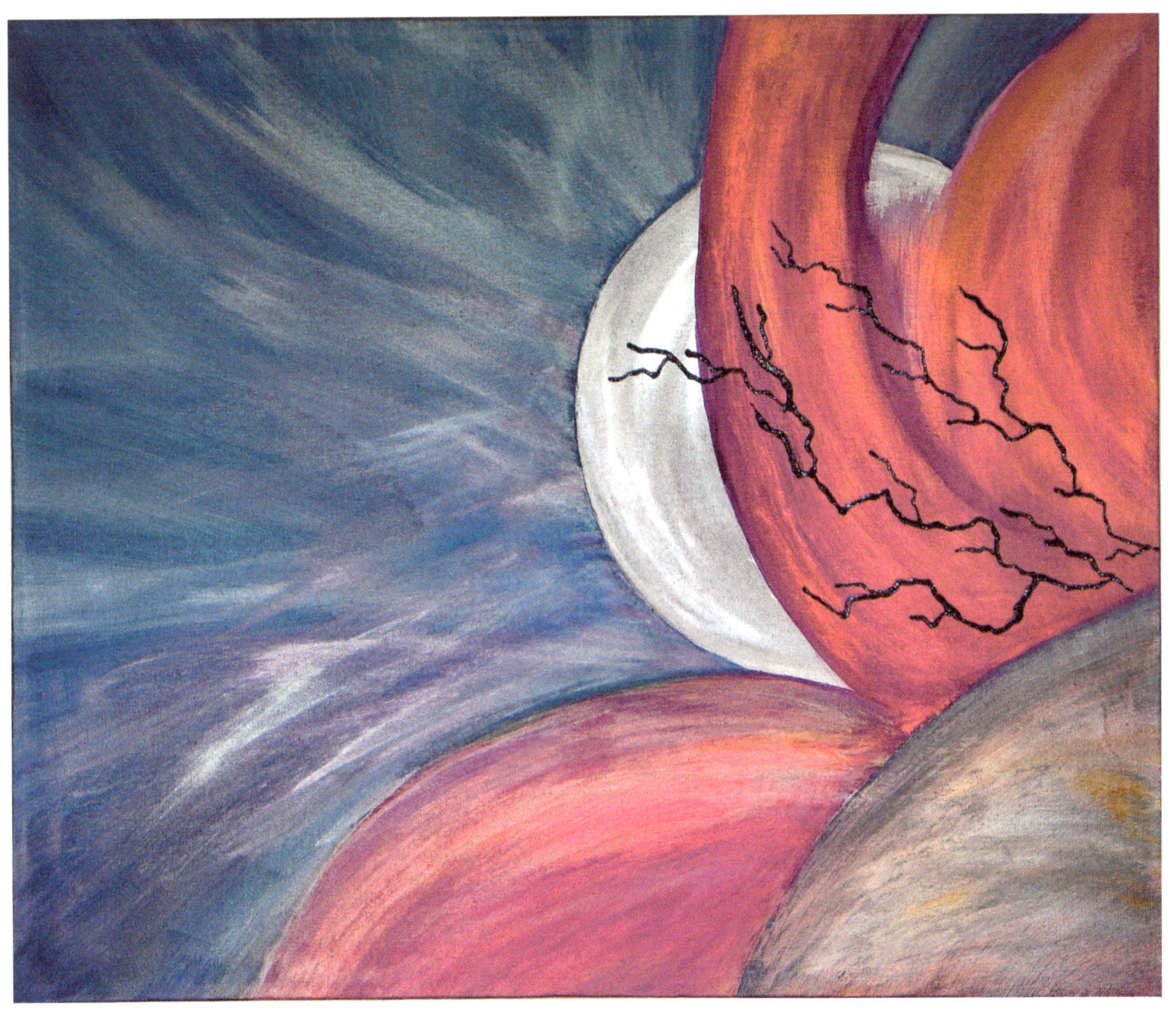

FLOWERS & LIGHT

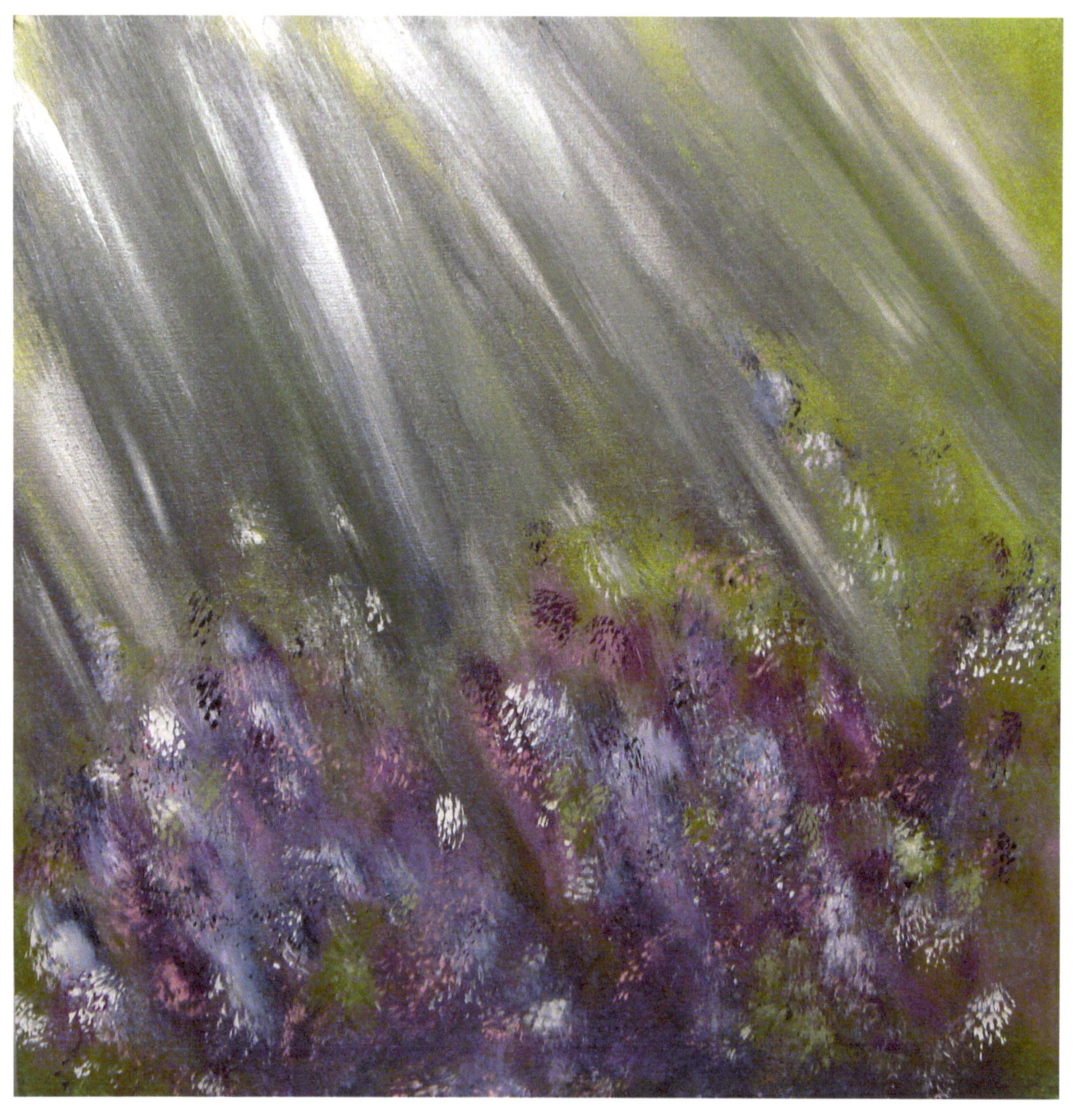

GHOST PLANETS

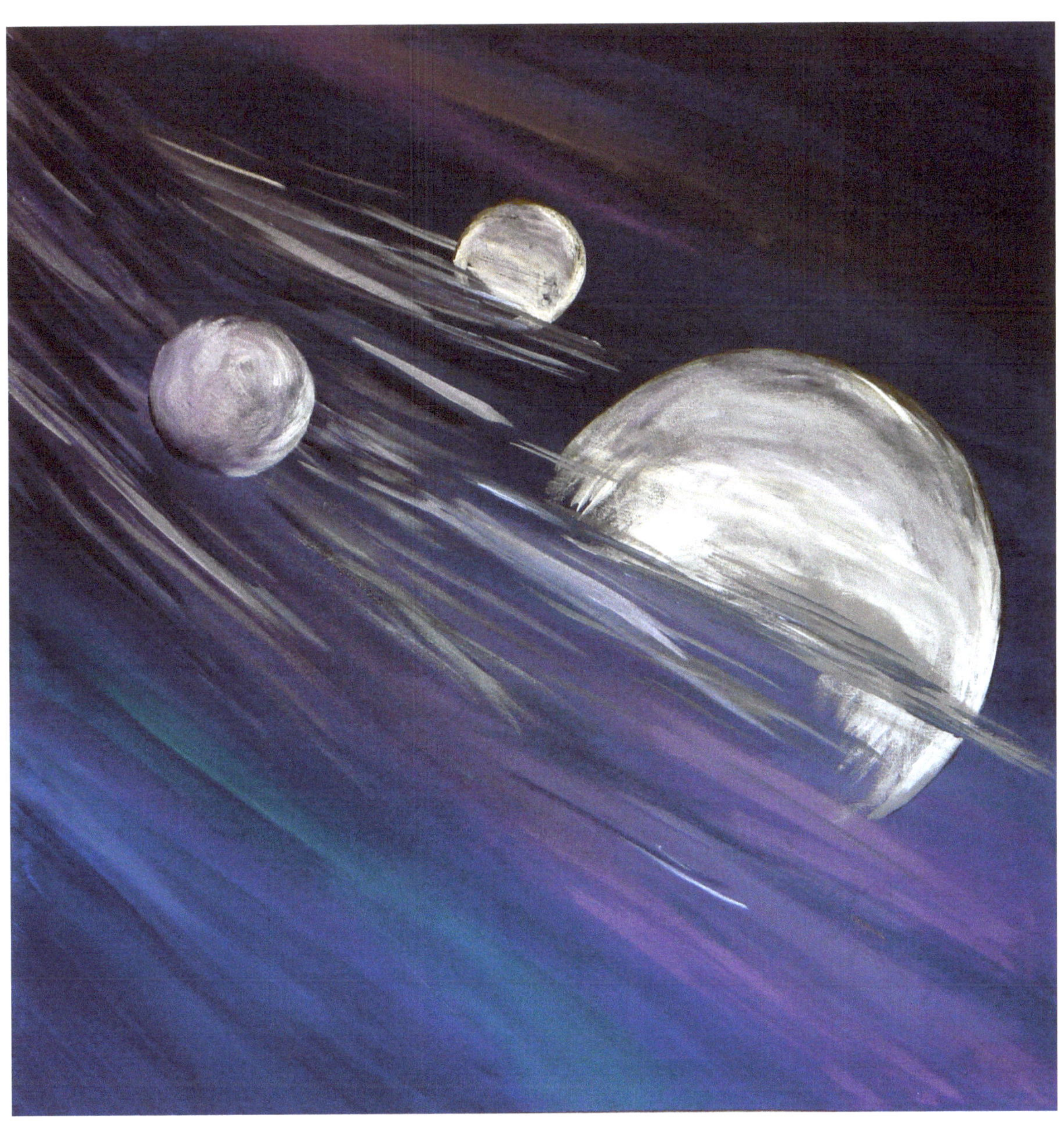

GENESIS

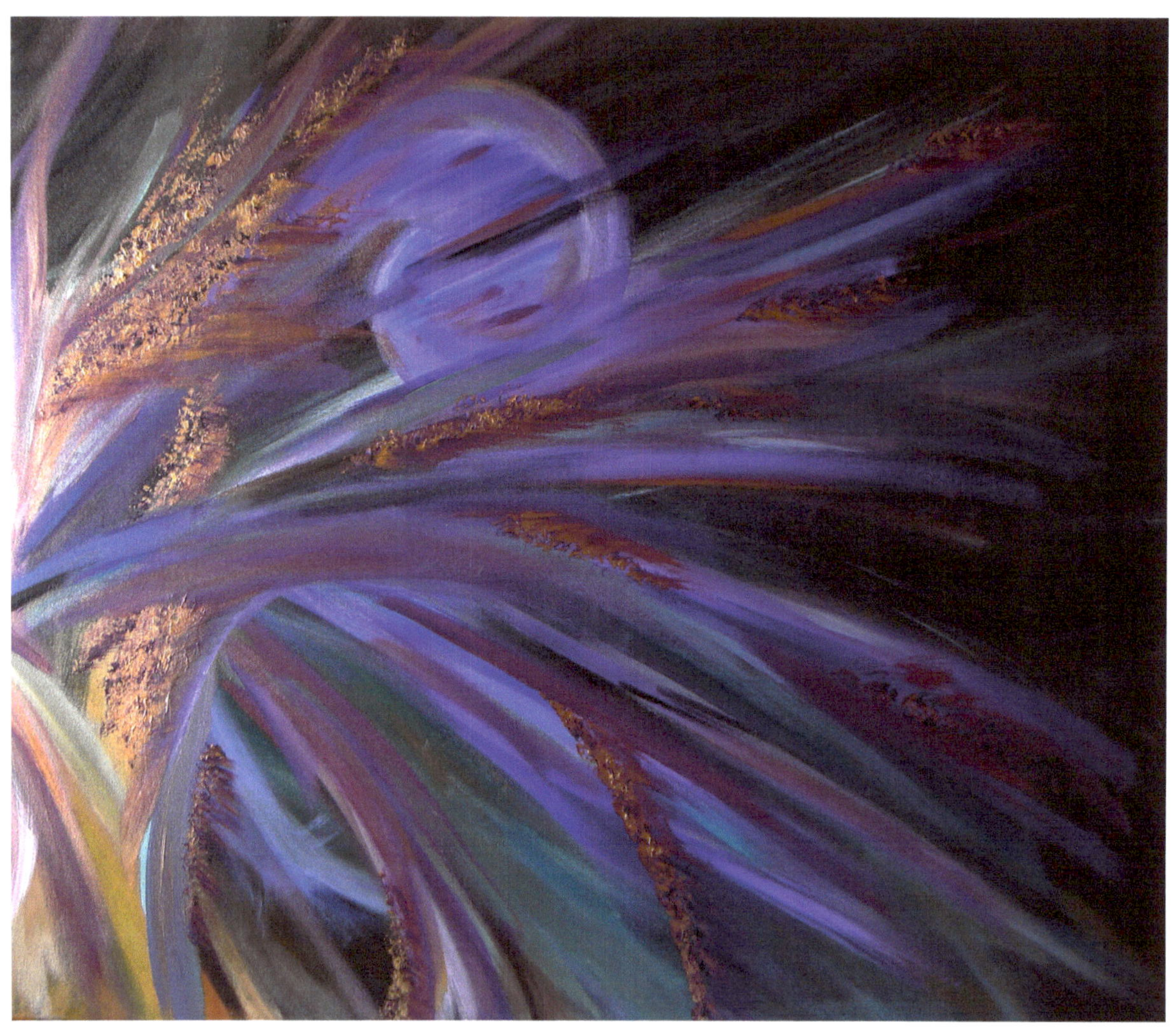

LADY HAWK

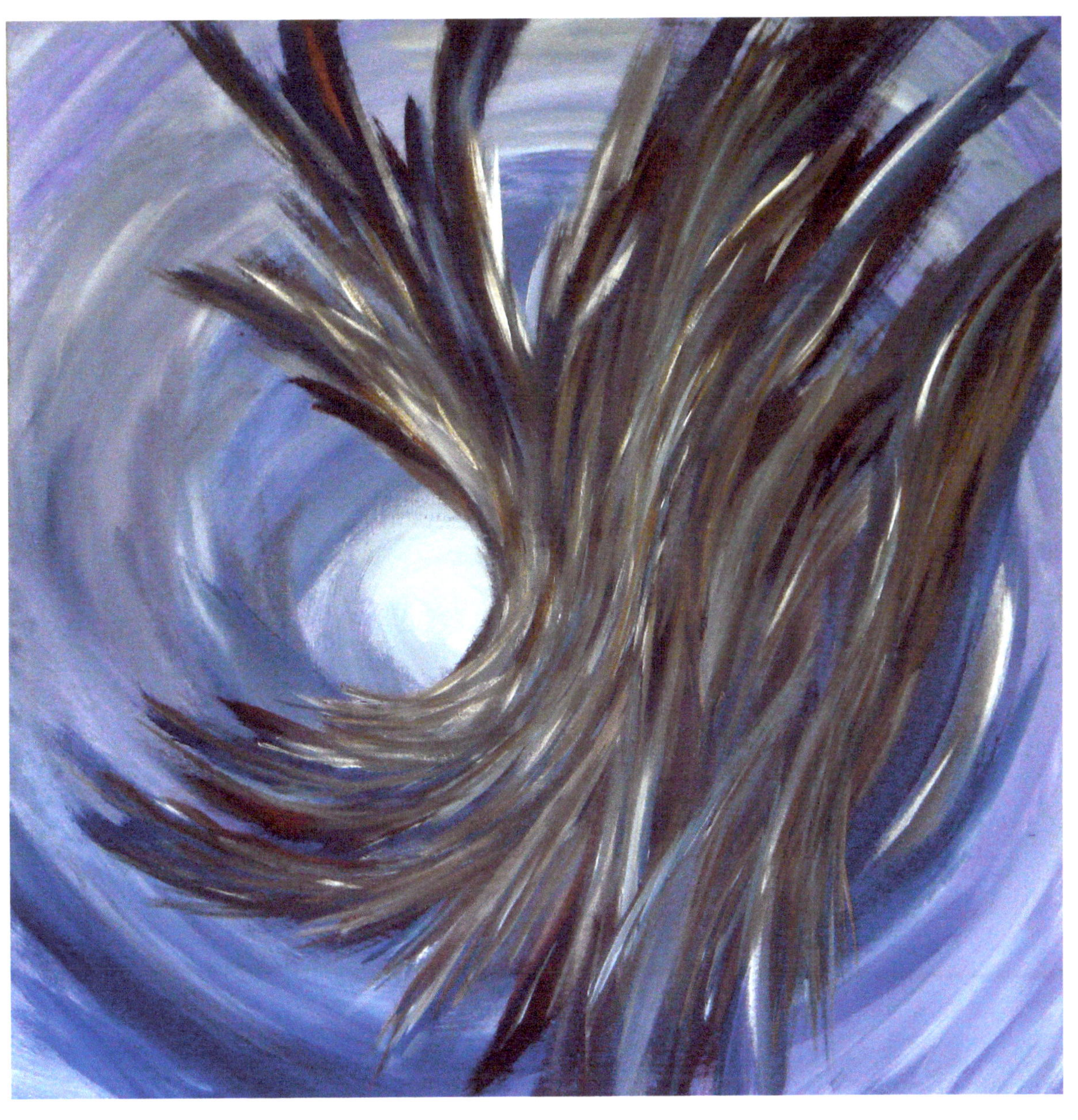

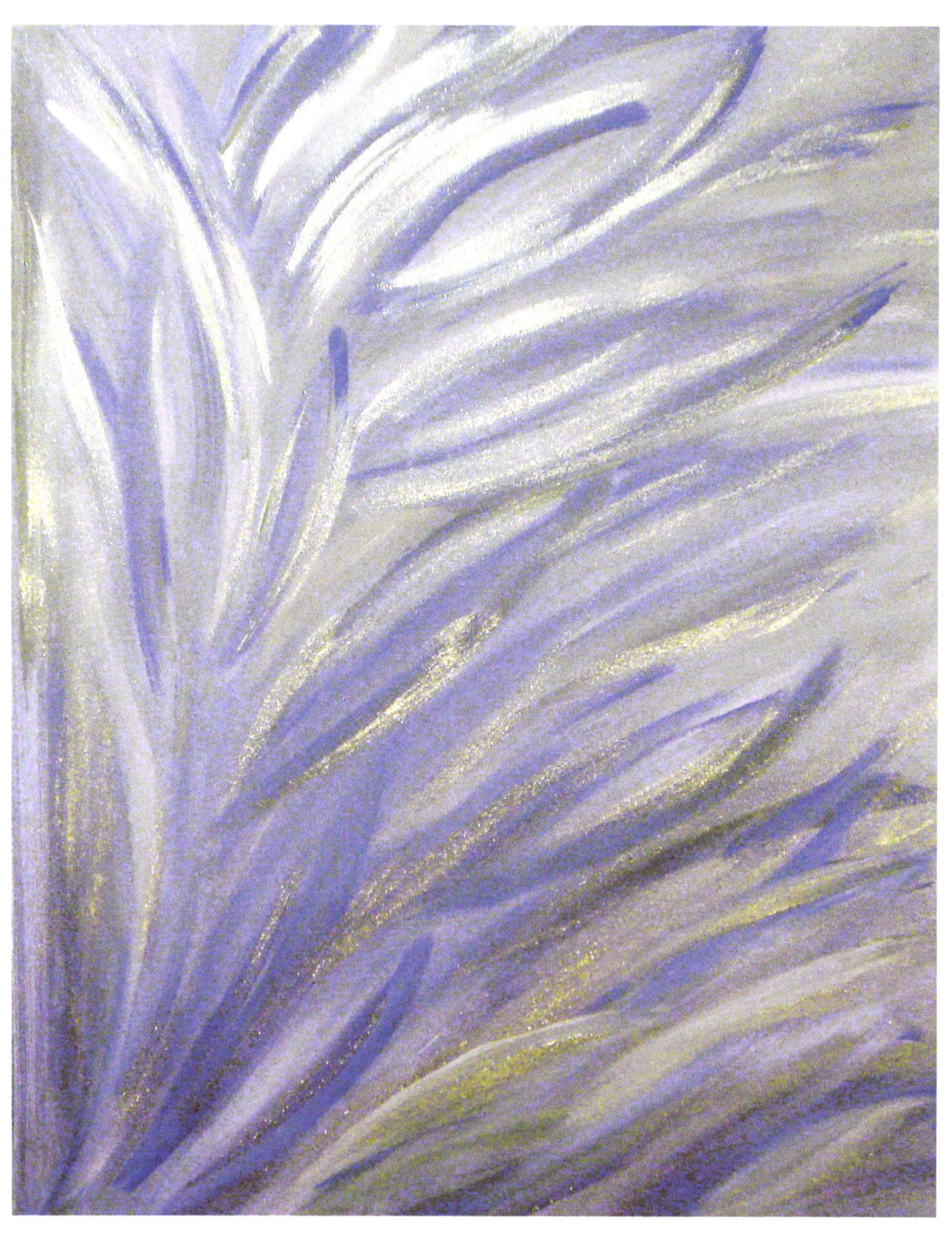

MAGIC

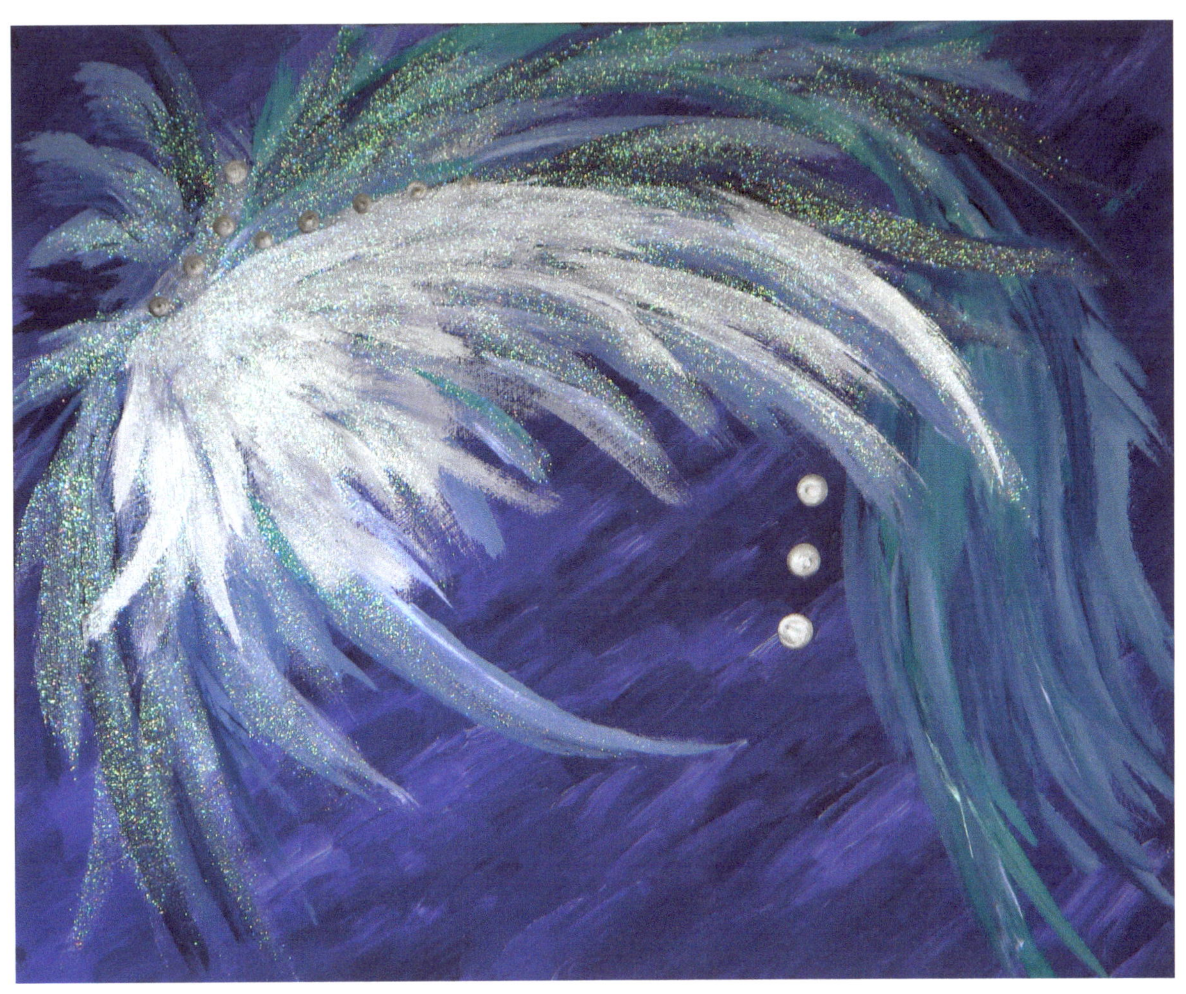

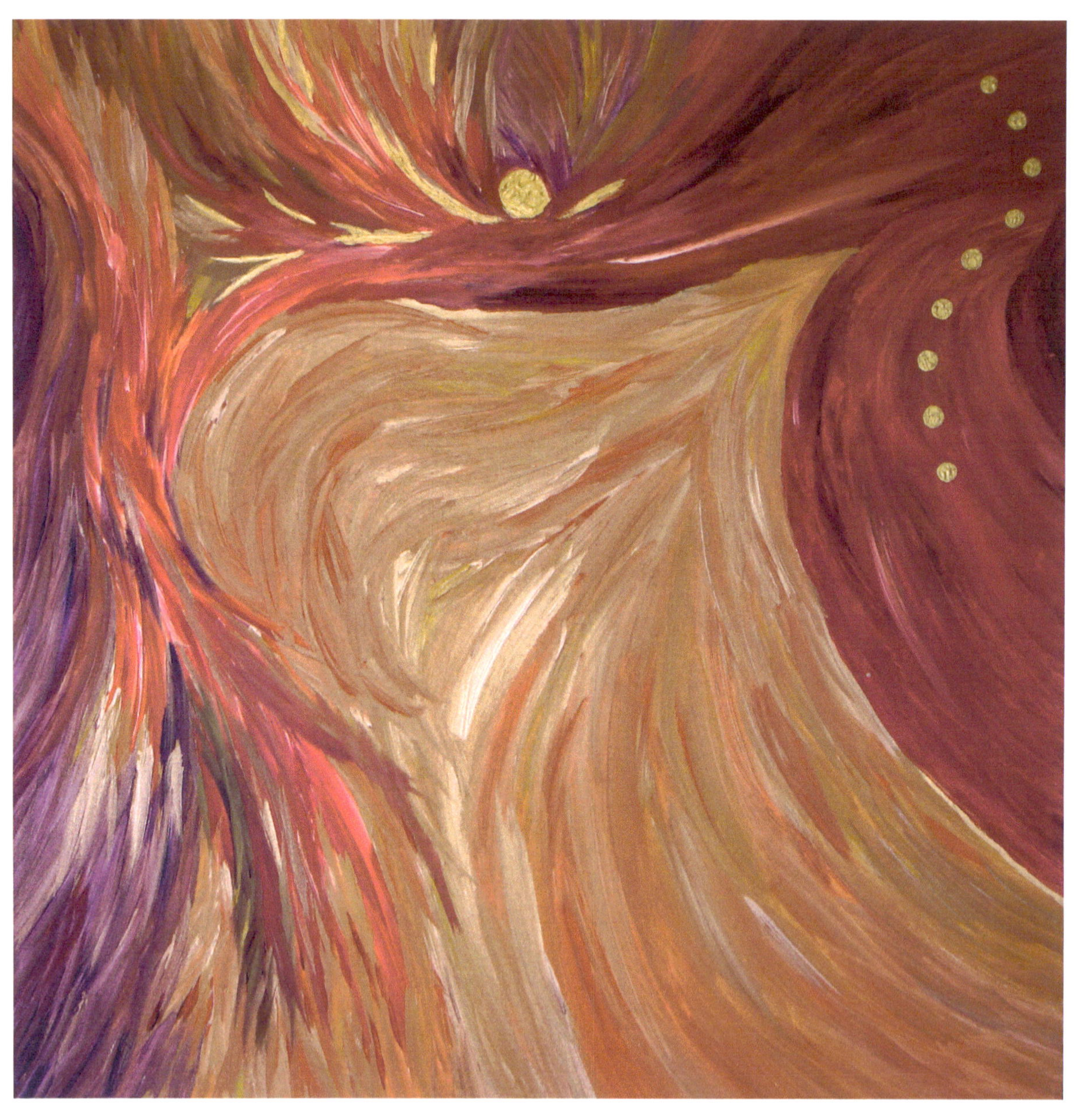

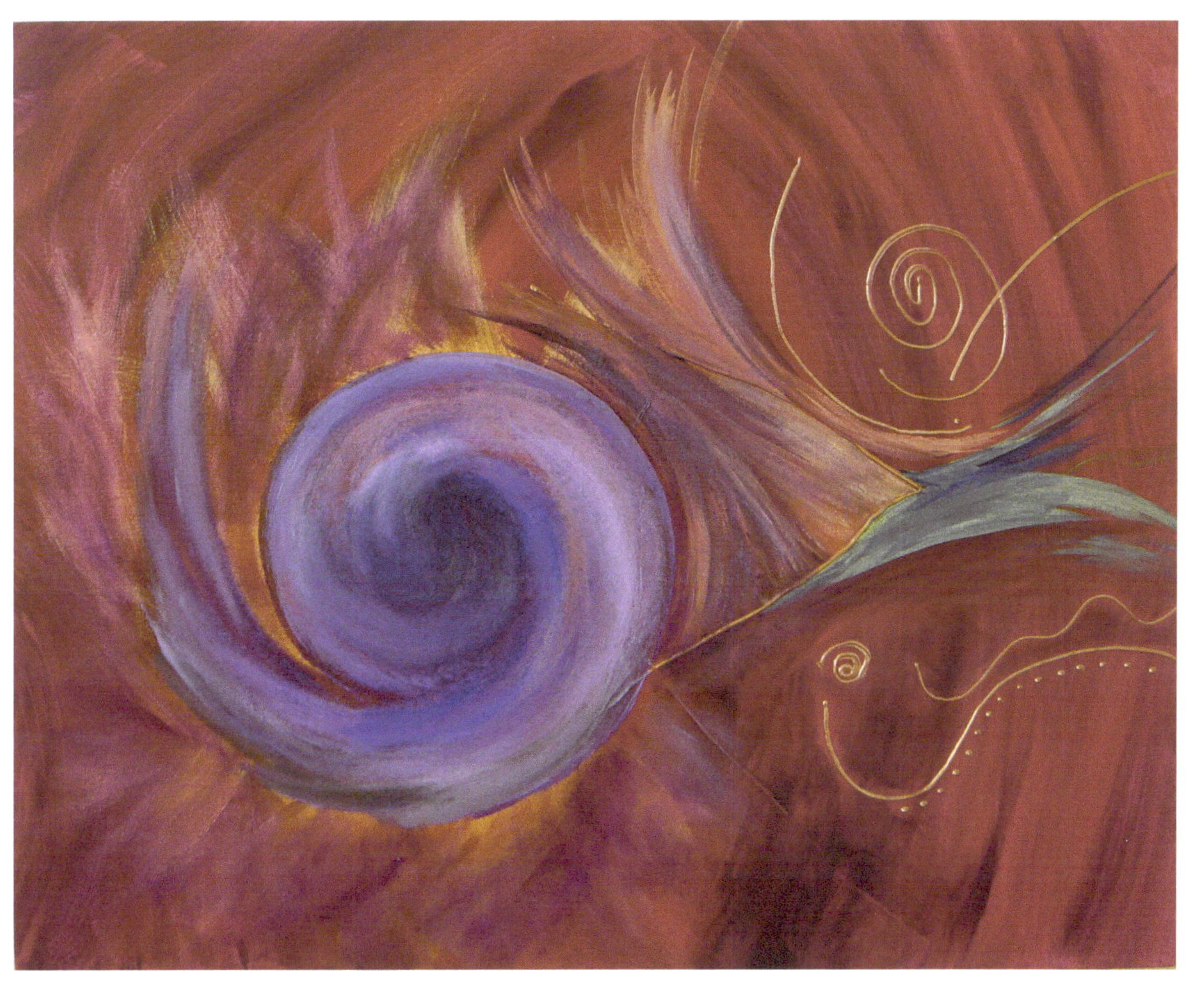

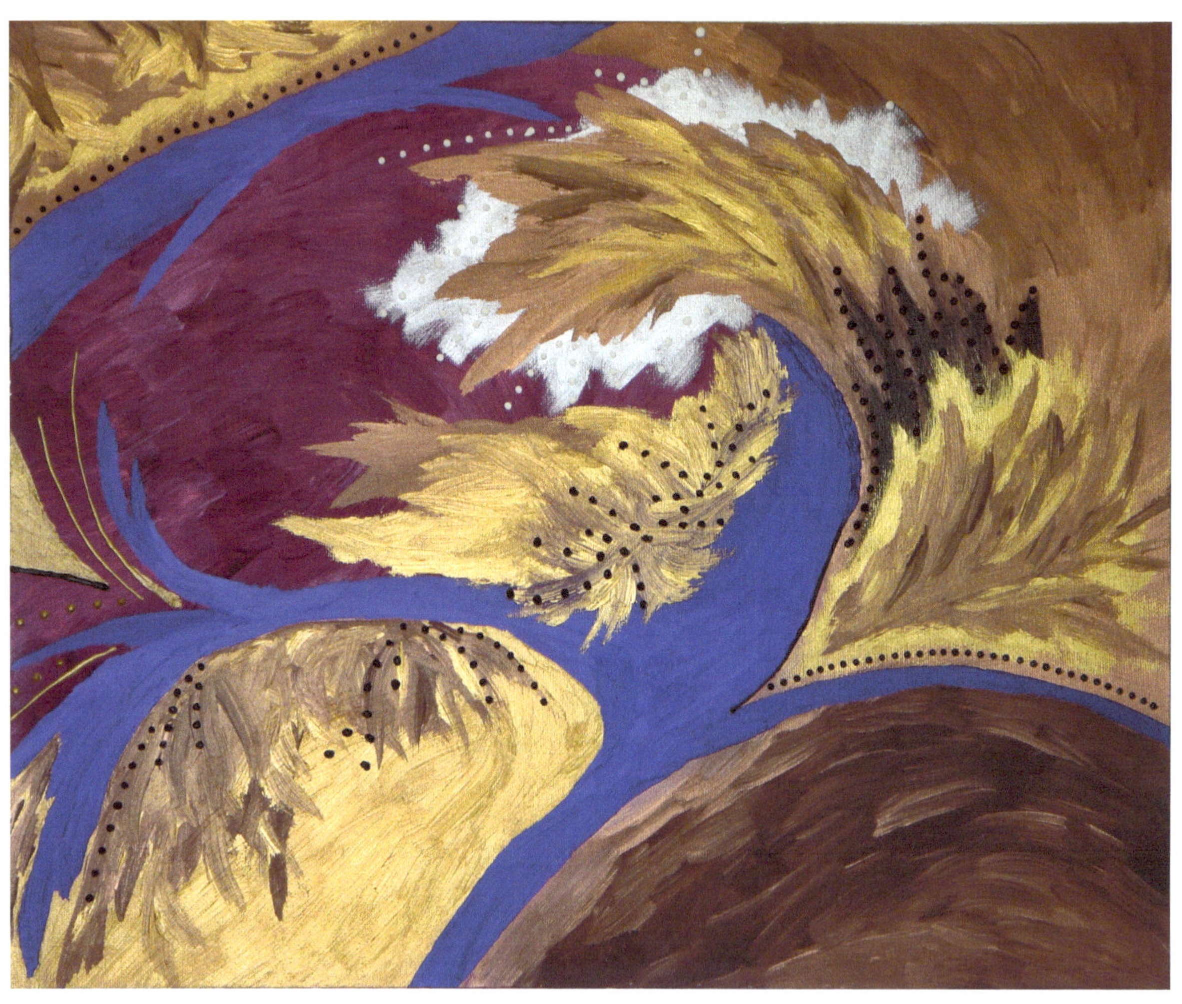

THE BLUE PHOENIX

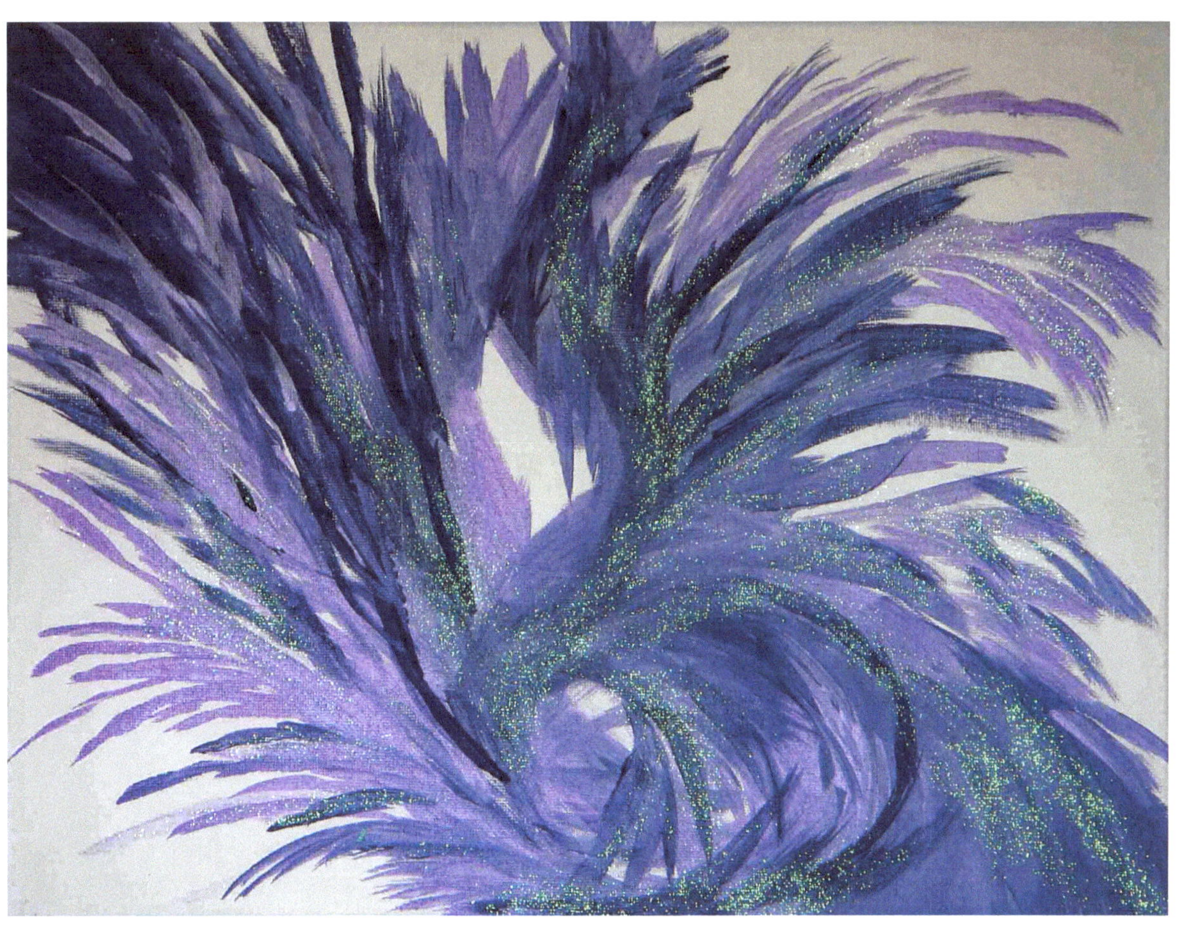

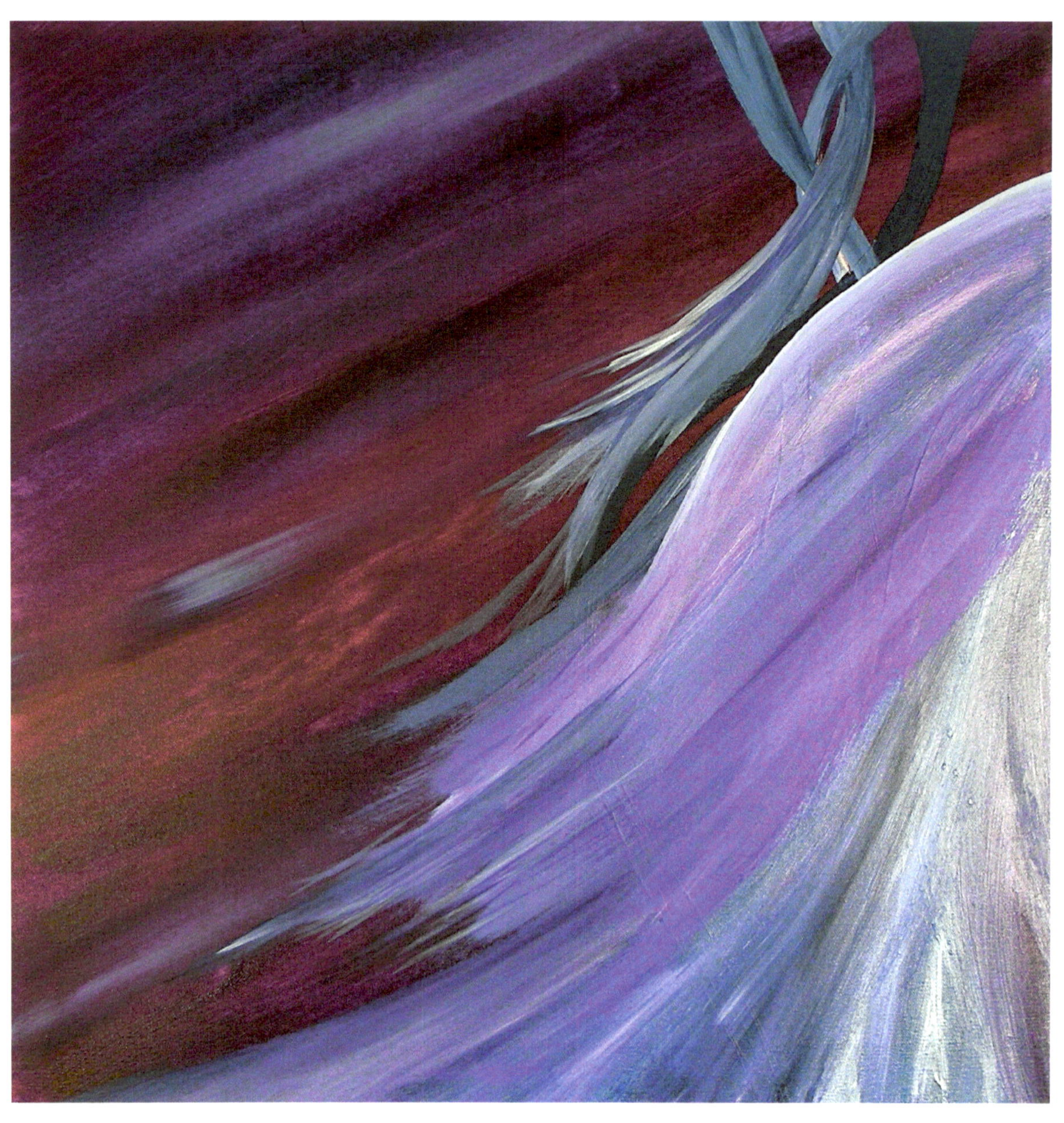

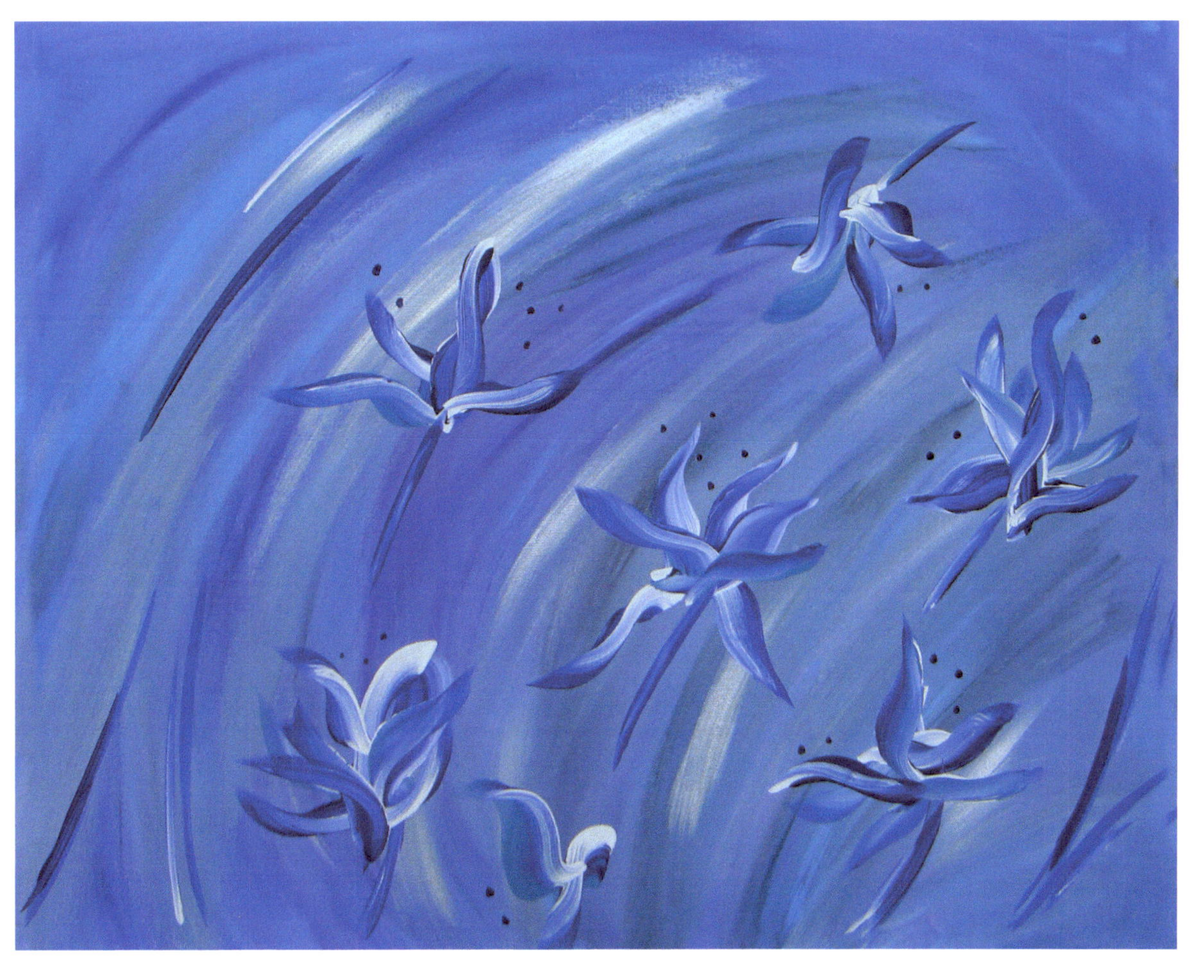

THE MANTLE

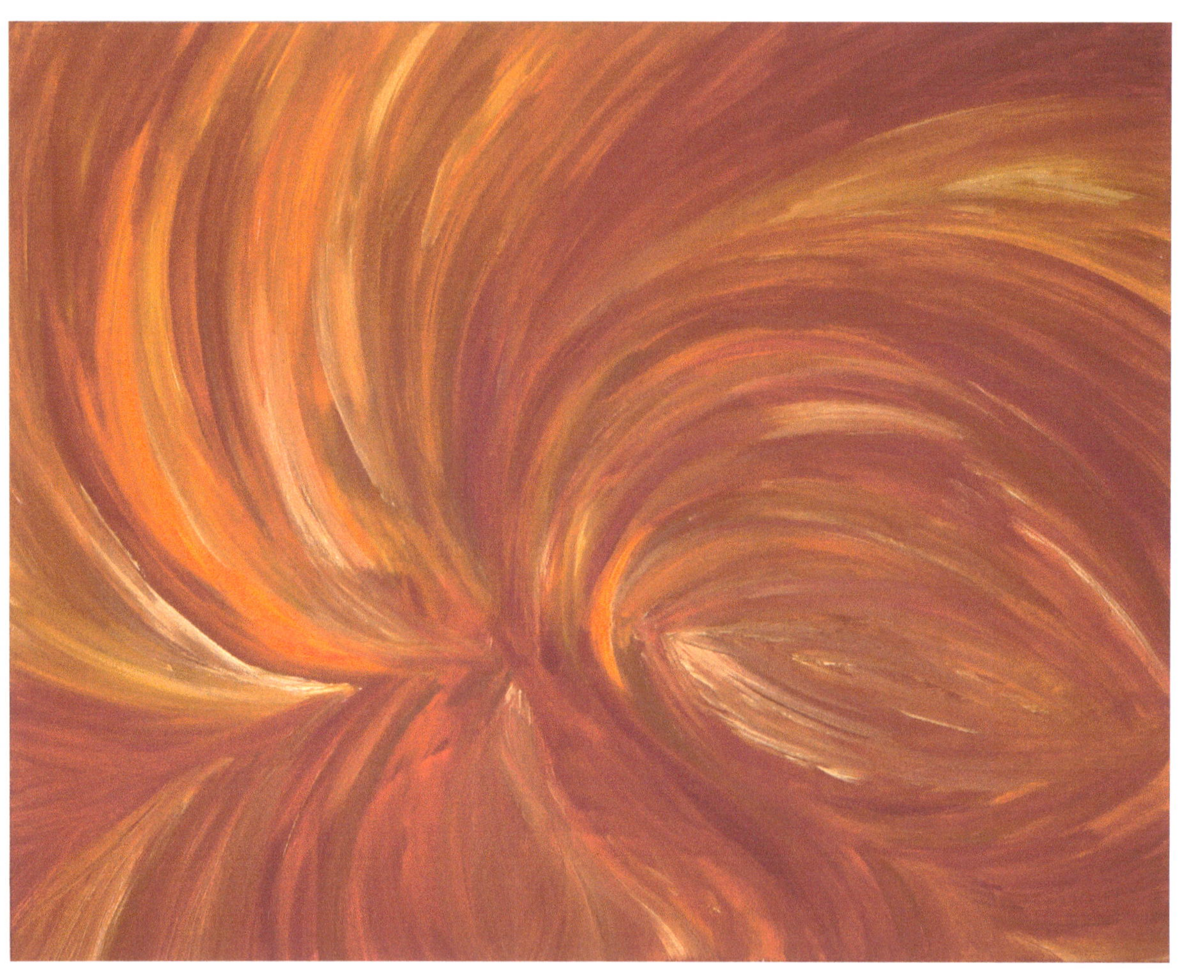

WILDFIRE FLOWERS

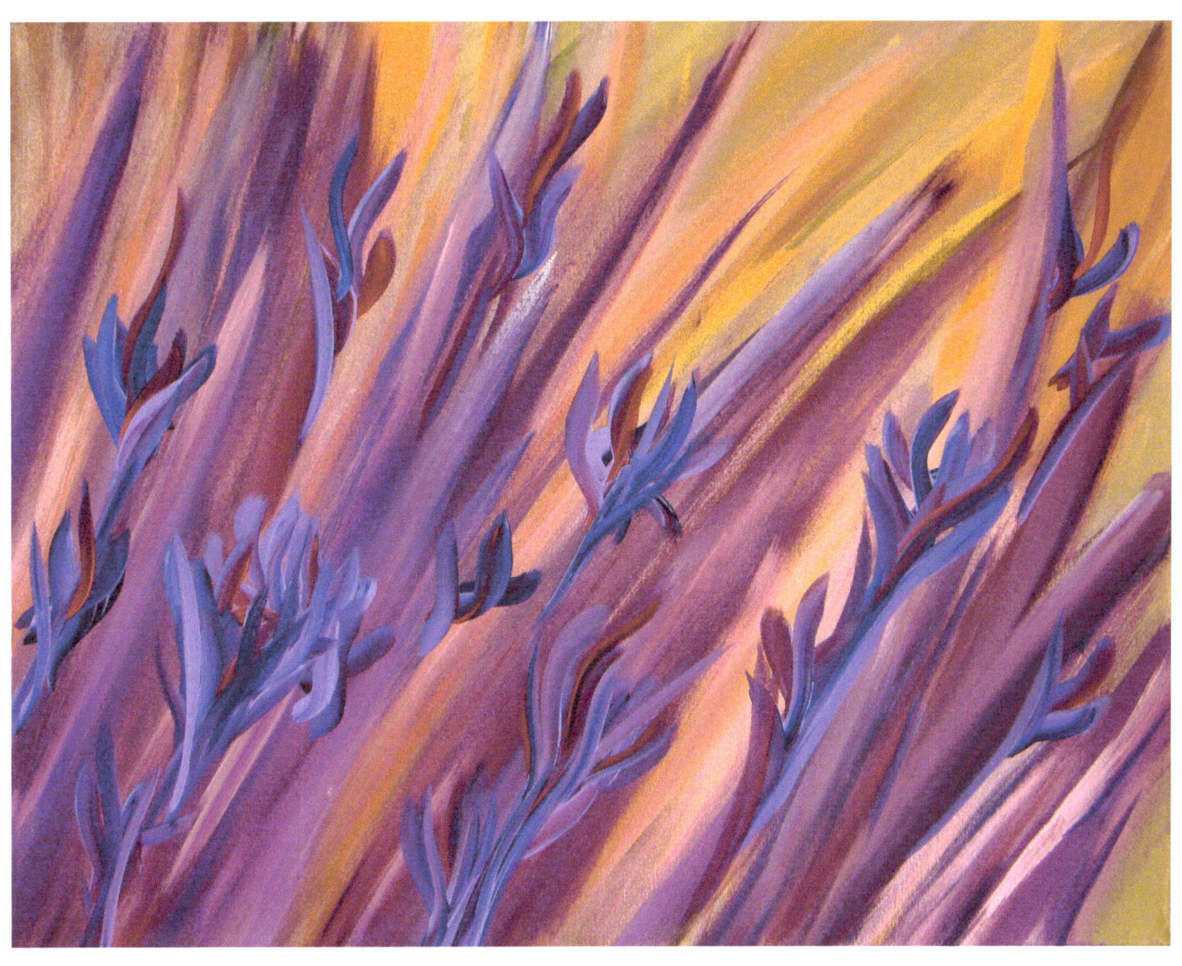

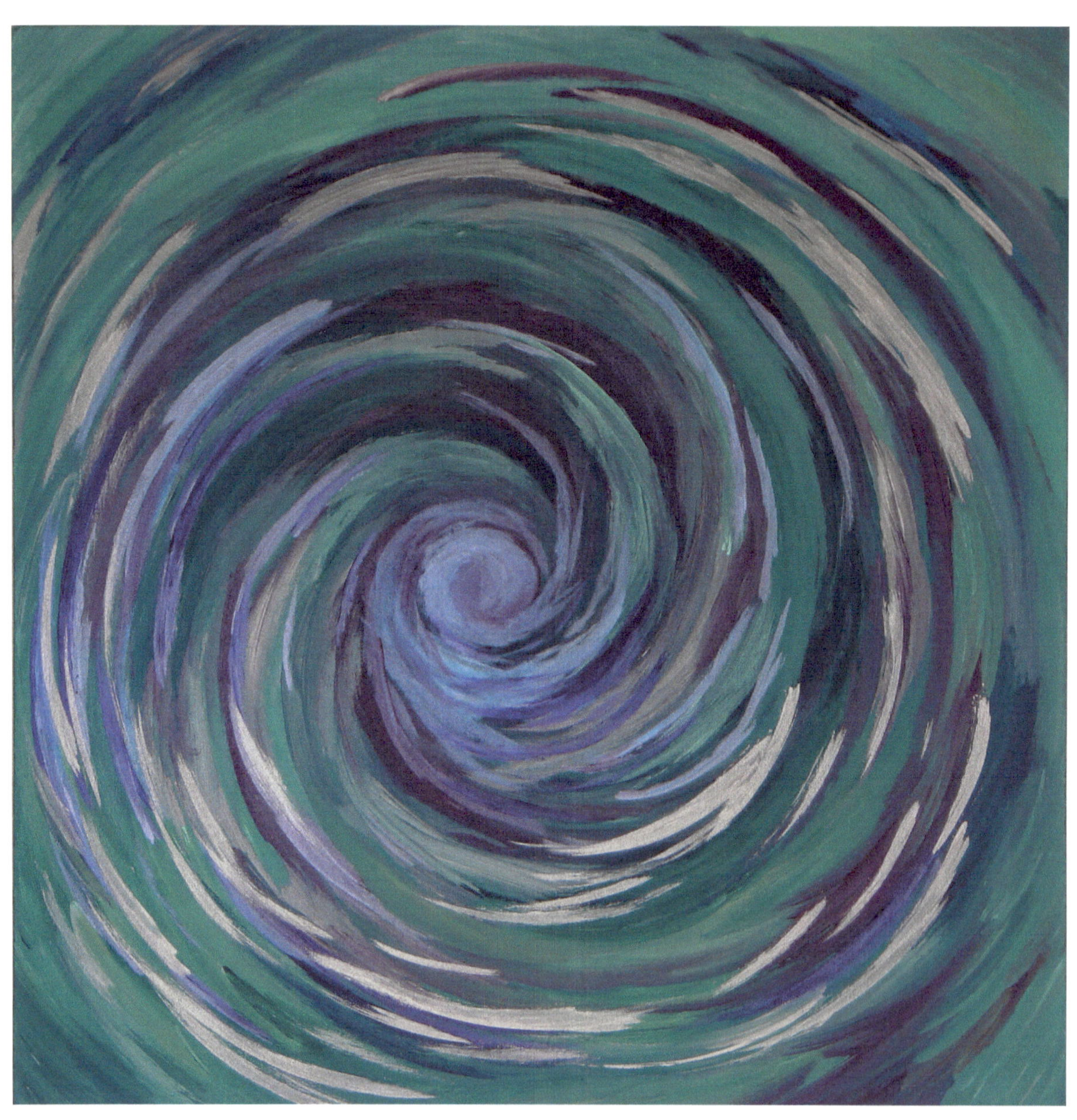

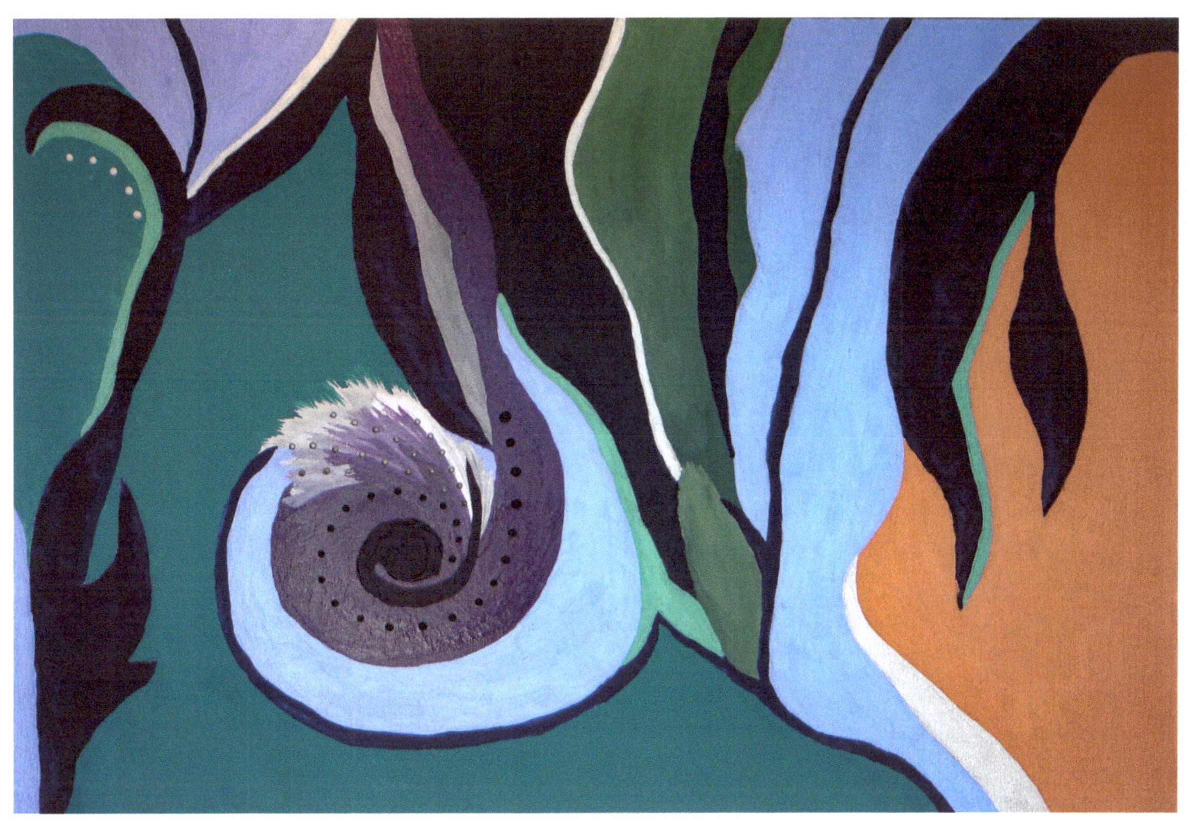

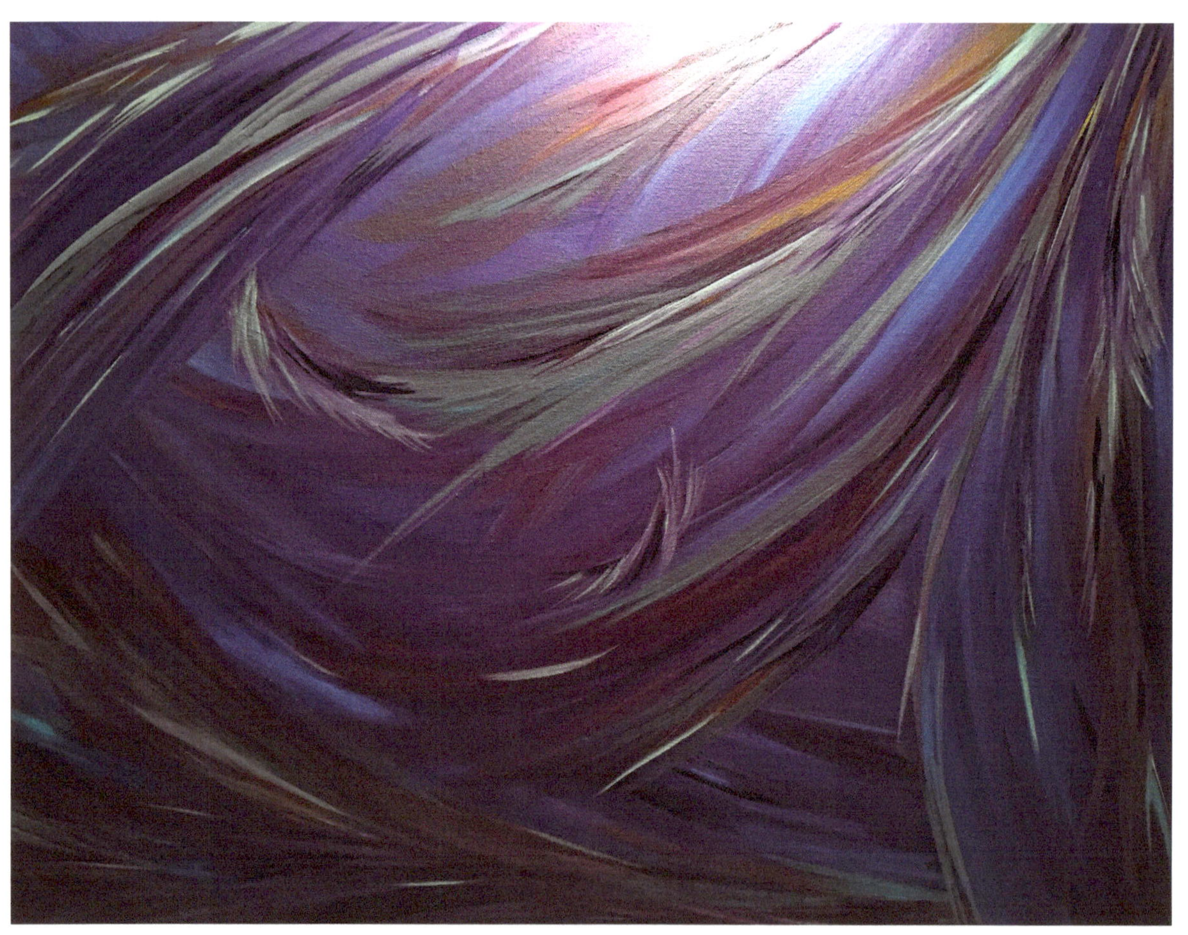

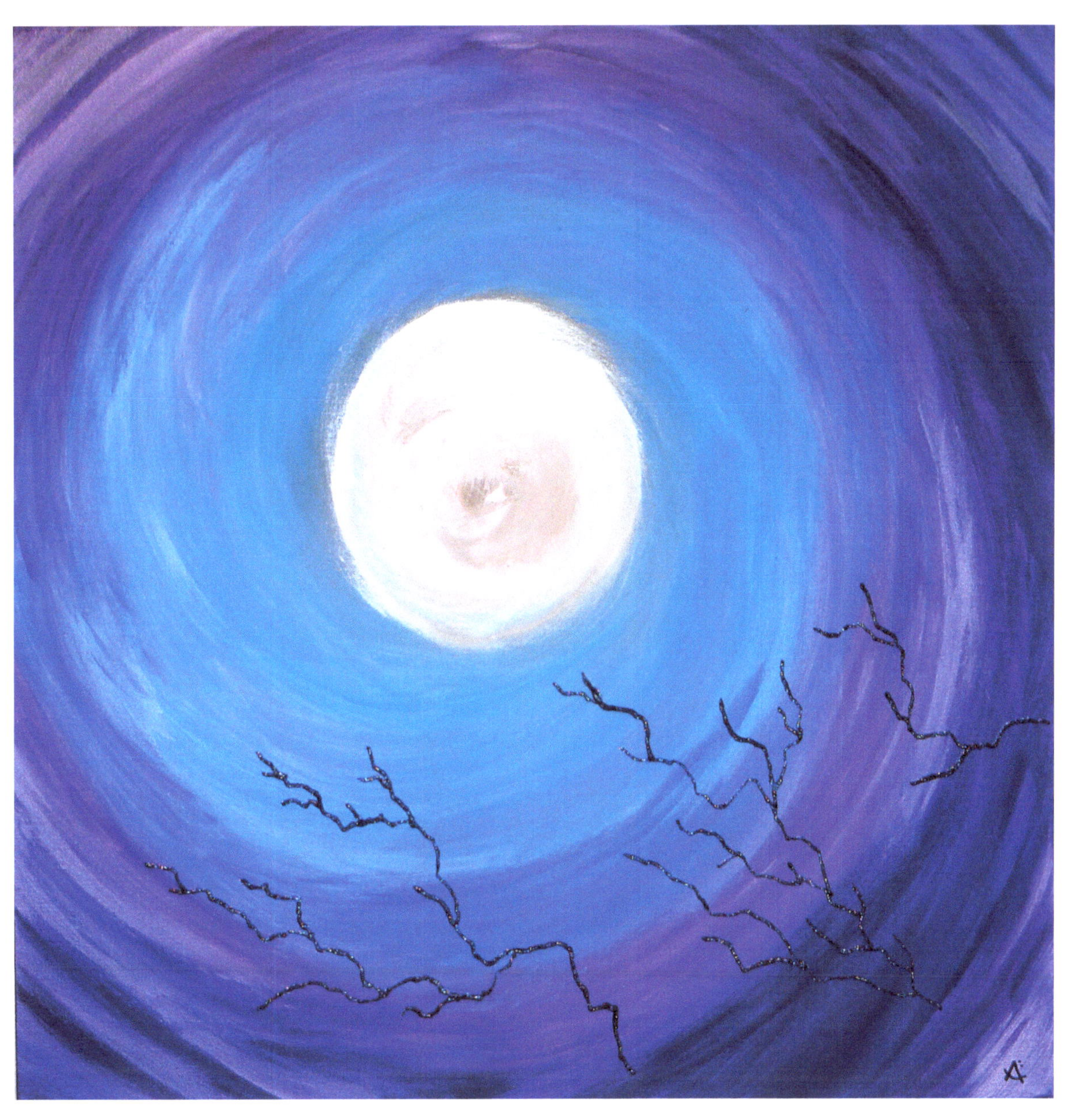

UNIVERSAL HARMONICS

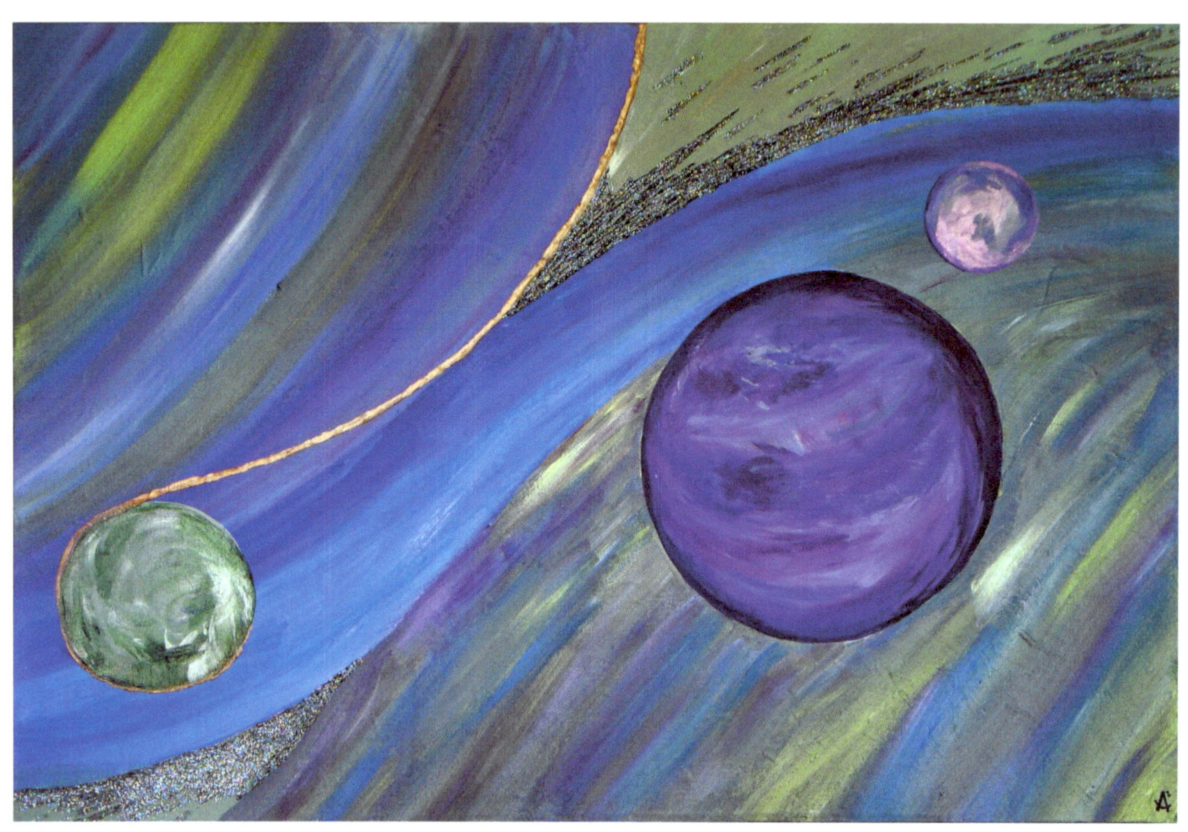

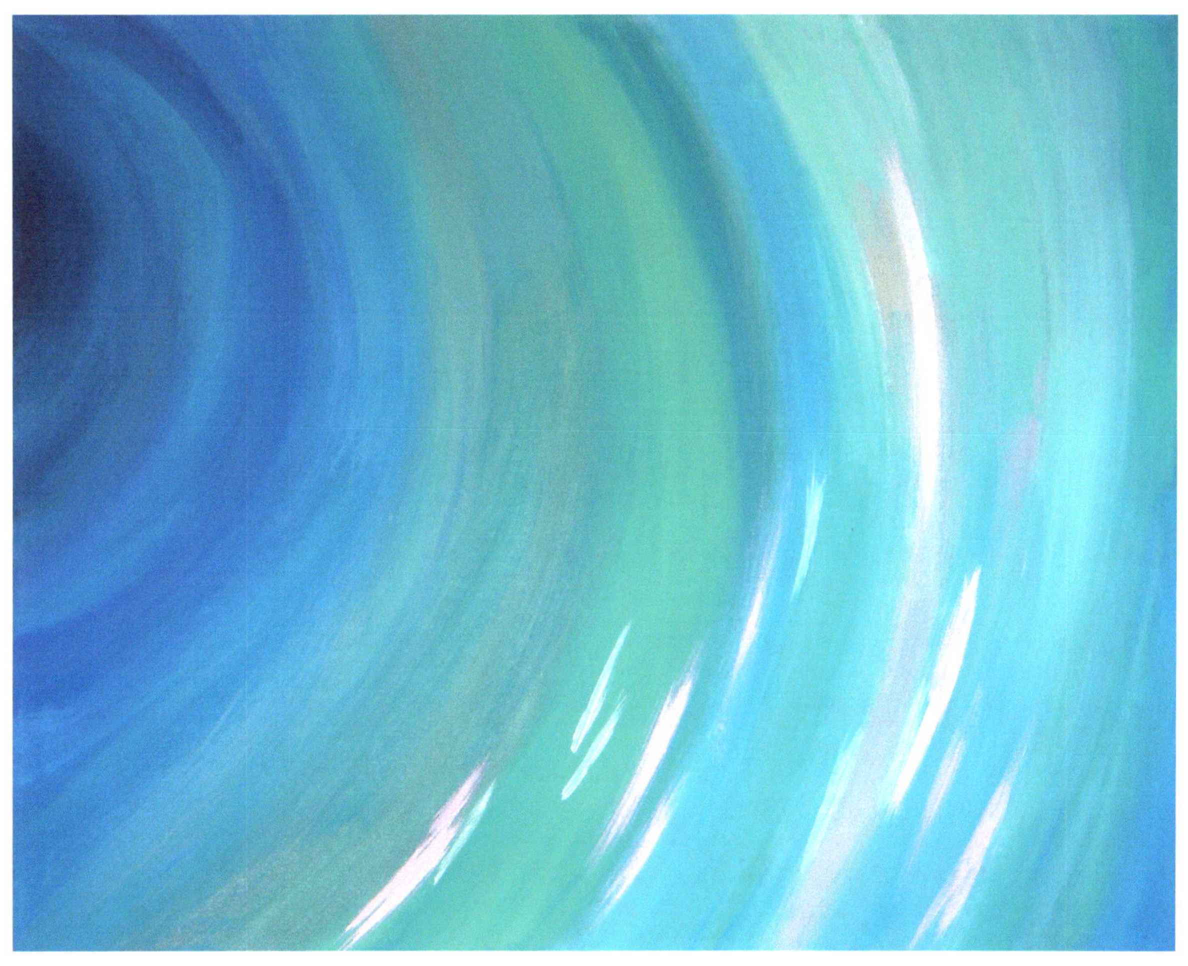